Smithsonian

LITTLE EXPLORER

VOLCANOES

by Martha E. H. Rustad

CAPSTONE PRESS
a capstone imprint

Little Explorer is published by Capstone Press,
1710 Roe Crest Drive, North Mankato, Minnesota 56003
www.capstonepub.com

Library of Congress Cataloging-in-Publication Data
Rustad, Martha E. H. (Martha Elizabeth Hillman), 1975– author.
  Volcanoes / by Martha E. H. Rustad.
pages cm. — (Smithsonian Little explorer)
Summary: "Introduces the science of volcanoes to young readers,
including geologic formation, famous volcanoes, predicting
eruptions, and more"— Provided by publisher.
  Includes index.
  ISBN 978-1-4765-3934-8 (library binding)
  ISBN 978-1-4765-5182-1 (paperback)
  ISBN 978-1-4765-5270-5 (paper over board)
1. Volcanoes—Juvenile literature. I. Title.
QE521.3.R875 2014
551.21—dc23   2013032352

Editorial Credits

Kristen Mohn, editor; Sarah Bennett, designer; Marcie Spence,
media researcher; Danielle Ceminsky, production specialist

Our very special thanks to Paul Kimberly, Geologist/IT Specialist,
Office of the Associate Director for Science, National Museum of
Natural History, Smithsonian Institution, for his curatorial review.
Capstone would also like to thank Kealy Wilson, Smithsonian
Institution Project Coordinator and Product Development
Manager, and the following at Smithsonian Enterprises: Ellen
Nanney, Licensing Manager; Brigid Ferraro, Director of Licensing;
Carol LeBlanc, Senior Vice President, Consumer & Education
Products.

Image Credits

Alamy: Classic Image, 27 (top), Everett Collection, 5 (top left),
Haraldur Stefansson, 13 (top), National Geographic Images
Collection, 28 (bottom), 29 (bottom), RGB Ventures LLC dba
SuperStock, 11 (bottom right), Tom Uhlman, 17 (bottom); Corbis:
Gary Braasch, 4-5, Lawson Wood, 11 (top), Luis Robayo/AFP,
17 (top), Reuters, 15 (bottom); Newscom: 14 (bottom), DEA/C.
Dani-i. Jeske Universal Images Group, 21 (top), Design Pics/
Huy Lam, 19 (top), Hallador Kolbeins/AFP/Getty Images, 15
(top), Johnny Wagner/ZUMA Press, 28 (top), Marcel Mochet/
AFP, 27 (bottom), NASA/AFP/Getty Images, 21 (bottom right),
Rob Reichenfeld Dorling Kindersley, 10 (bottom); Paul Rockwood,
Artist, Courtesy National Park Service, Crater Lake National Park
Museum & Archive Collections, 23 (left); Shutterstock: Aaron
Rutten, 8, Alexey Kamenskiy, 30-31, 32, Ammit Jack, 18 (bottom),
Andrea Danti, 6-7, creative, 29 (top), Dan Lee, 20, Designua, 9,
Dori Landwehrle, 21 (bottom left), Dr_Flash, 5 (middle), edelia,
26 (bottom), Fredy Thuerig 13 (bottom), Graeme Shannon, 22,
Jeff Banke, 23 (right), Lee Prince, 25, Manamana, 4 (bottom), My
Good Images, 16, N.Minton, 24 (bottom right), Nickolay Stanev, 18
(top), Piotr Gatlik, 24 (left), PRILL, 24 (top right), Radoslaw Lecyk,
6 (bottom), Rudolf Tepfenhart, 11 (bottom left), Sergey SP, 19
(bottom), Sunshine Pics, cover, suronin, 10 (top), Vulkanette, 1, 12,
Yurumi, design element; Wikipedia: NASA, 14 (top), Rolfsteiner,
26 (top), USGS/Carol Spears, 5 (top right)

For Markus, my budding volcanologist. —MEHR

Printed in the United States of America in North Mankato, Minnesota.
040115   008873R

TABLE OF CONTENTS

MOUNT ST. HELENS

Magma pushes up. A cloud of ash puffs out. A volcano explodes.

Mount St. Helens was quiet for 123 years. But it erupted on May 18, 1980.

The eruption blasted away the mountain's peak. Ash clouds blocked out the sun.

Volcanology is the study of volcanoes. Scientists such as geologists, biologists, and meteorologists also study volcanoes.

before

after

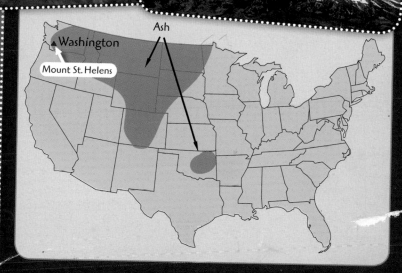

Washington

Mount St. Helens

Ash

Winds blew ash as far as Minnesota and Oklahoma.

WHAT IS A VOLCANO?

A volcano is a hill or mountain with a hole at the top called a crater.

Gases and ash rise into the air when a volcano erupts.

Melted rock blasts or pours out through the crater.

Lava pushes out through vents.

Side vents are craters on the sides of a volcano.

A **vent** is another name for a hole in Earth's crust.

Hot lava glows red. Its temperature can reach 2,200 degrees Fahrenheit (1,200 degrees Celsius). It turns black when it cools.

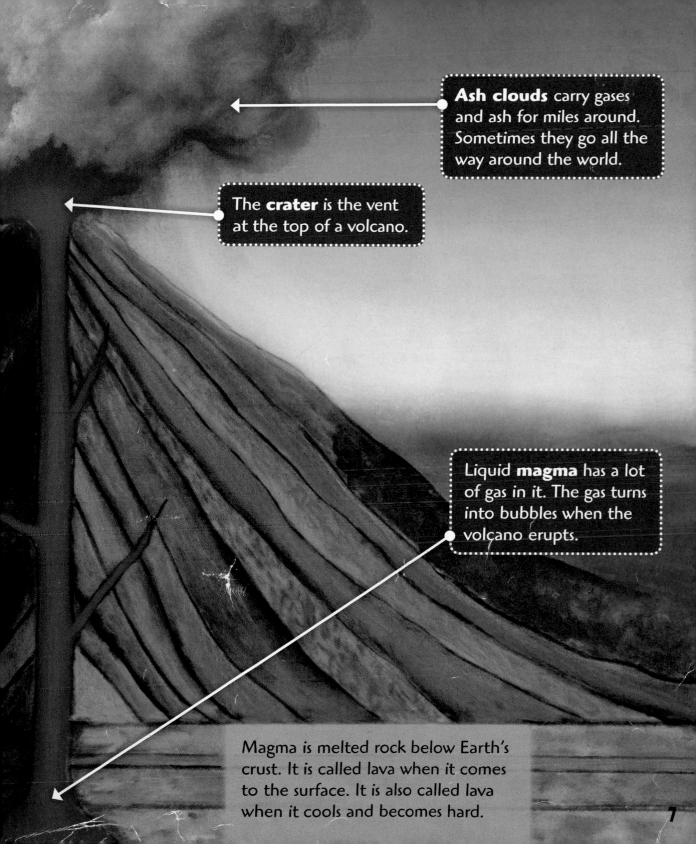

Ash clouds carry gases and ash for miles around. Sometimes they go all the way around the world.

The **crater** is the vent at the top of a volcano.

Liquid **magma** has a lot of gas in it. The gas turns into bubbles when the volcano erupts.

Magma is melted rock below Earth's crust. It is called lava when it comes to the surface. It is also called lava when it cools and becomes hard.

7

LAYERS OF EARTH

Planet Earth has three main layers.

We live on the **CRUST**.

Under the crust lies the **MANTLE**.
Pressure and heat create magma in the mantle. This causes volcanoes to form on the crust above.

The **CORE** is in the middle.
Temperatures inside the core may reach 10,000°F (5,500°C). The sun's surface is about the same temperature. It is so hot that rocks melt.

Layer	Thickness
Crust	as much as 30 miles (50 kilometers) thick
Mantle	1,800 miles (2,900 km) thick
Core	3,500 miles (5,600 km) thick

Plates are huge pieces of Earth's crust.
They fit together like a puzzle.

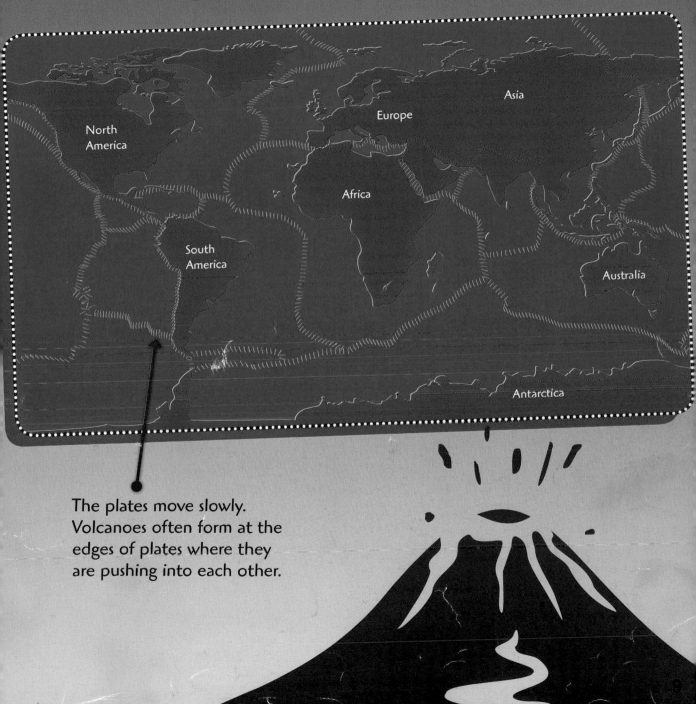

North
America

Europe

Asia

Africa

South
America

Australia

Antarctica

The plates move slowly.
Volcanoes often form at the
edges of plates where they
are pushing into each other.

KINDS OF VOLCANOES

Stratovolcanoes look like giant cones. Ash and lava build up over time to form their steep sides. A crater sits at the top.

Gentle slopes form the sides of **shield volcanoes**. The flow of lava hardens to form a flattened dome.

Submarine volcanoes erupt underwater. Lava cools quickly in ocean water. The top of the volcano can break the surface of the ocean. A new island is born.

A **fissure volcano** cracks Earth's crust open in a long line. Iceland's Laki erupted in 1783. The crack was 15 miles (24 km) long. Lava, ash, and gases spewed out for nine months. The ash reached as far as northern Africa.

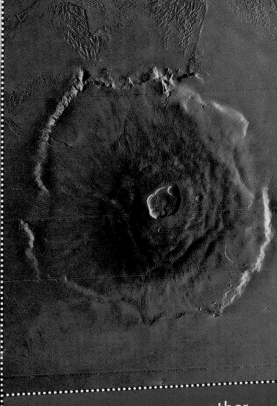

There are volcanoes on other planets. Olympus Mons is a large volcano on Mars.

ERUPTIONS

All volcanic eruptions are not the same.

Some eruptions are violent explosions.
Ash, lava, and steam burst out. The
eruption might be over in a few minutes
or a few hours. Or it might last many days.

In 2010 a volcano nicknamed Eyja (pronounced AY-ya) erupted in Iceland. Ash poured into the sky for a week. Wind carried the ash across the Atlantic ocean. Airplanes across Europe could not fly for many days.

Other times lava flows slowly from volcanoes. Waves of molten rock flow for days or even months.

VOLCANO DANGERS

Ash clouds block sunlight.

Some eruptions kill people and destroy buildings.

Very large eruptions change the weather even far away.

In 1815 Mount Tambora erupted in Indonesia. Ash clouds darkened the sky. Temperatures worldwide dropped by about 5°F (3°C). The following year was still cool. People called it "the year without a summer."

Clouds of toxic gases and ash kill crops.

Volcano eruptions at sea make big waves.

Tsunamis also happen when big volcanic rocks fall into the ocean.

OTHER DANGERS

Imagine a volcano peak covered with snow.
What happens when the volcano erupts?

A big avalanche crashes down the mountain.

A lahar is a mixture of lava, rock, mud, and other rubble. It flows down the sides of volcanoes.

A lahar knocks over everything in its path.

lahar damage to a road

HOW VOLCANOES HELP

Our planet needs volcanoes. Pressure builds up inside Earth. Volcanoes let the pressure out.

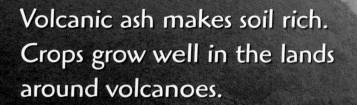

Volcanic ash makes soil rich.
Crops grow well in the lands
around volcanoes.

Lava that cools quickly makes obsidian.
Sharp tools and arrows can be made
from this glasslike rock.

FROM LAVA TO LAND

When hot lava cools, hard rock is left.
New islands rise up and grow larger from volcanoes.

Earth's newest island may be in the Red Sea.
A volcano erupted in the Zubair Island chain.
This island formed in 2011. It is not yet named.

Volcanoes made all the Hawaiian Islands. Mauna Loa,
on the Big Island of Hawaii, is Earth's largest volcano.
Hawaii's Kilauea is one of the most active volcanoes.

Mauna Loa volcanoes

Hawaiian Island of Kauai

DORMANT VOLCANOES

Dormant volcanoes are quiet. They have not erupted for hundreds or thousands of years.

Mount Kilamanjaro rises 19,340 feet (5,895 m) above Africa. Three volcanoes make up this mountain. The last big eruption here was 360,000 years ago.

Our planet has about 1,500 active volcanoes. As many as 25 erupt every day. Another 500 volcanoes are dormant.

A huge eruption rocked Mount Mazama in Oregon about 7,000 years ago.

The top of the volcano caved in. Rainwater and snow filled the deep hole. Crater Lake formed.

Crater Lake

Dormant volcanoes might erupt again someday.

GEOTHERMAL ENERGY

Geothermal means heat from inside Earth.

Magma heats underground water. The hot water bubbles up from hot springs.

hot springs

geothermal power station

People in Iceland use geothermal energy to heat and power their homes.

Whoosh! A geyser spouts from the ground.

Steam and hot water burst into the air.

Old Faithful is a geyser in Yellowstone National Park. It has erupted every hour or two for hundreds of years.

FAMOUS VOLCANOES

THERA

An eruption rocked the volcano Thera on a Greek island about 3,500 years ago. Ash and rocks traveled as far as Egypt. Stories about the lost city of Atlantis may have started here.

MOUNT VESUVIUS

Vesuvius is an active volcano in Italy. In the year AD 79, a huge eruption buried the city of Pompeii. About 2,000 people died.

"ASHES WERE ALREADY FALLING ... I LOOKED ROUND: A DENSE BLACK CLOUD WAS COMING UP BEHIND US, SPREADING OVER THE EARTH LIKE A FLOOD."

— Pliny the Younger, from a letter about the Mount Vesuvius eruption in AD 79

KRAKATAU

A huge eruption rocked Krakatau in August 1883. No one lived on this island in Indonesia. But tsunami waves hit Java and Sumatra. About 36,000 people died.

HEKLA

Iceland's Hekla erupts often. One eruption started in 1947 and lasted more than one year! Ash flew up more than 16 miles (26 km). The last eruption was in 2000.

PREDICTING ERUPTIONS

Volcanologists work hard to tell when a volcano will erupt.

They watch for ash clouds. They measure gases and earthquakes.

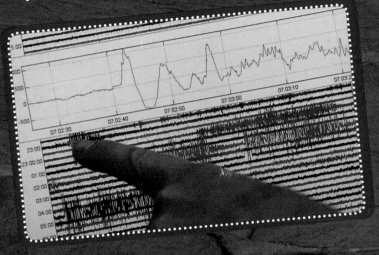

Small eruptions sometimes warn that a big eruption may happen.

People who live near volcanoes must watch for warnings.

In 1980 scientists warned people that Mount St. Helens might erupt. Small earthquakes rumbled. Steam came out. A bump formed on the side of the peak. Thousands of people evacuated. Fifty-seven people died.

GLOSSARY

ash—a powder that results from an explosion; ash comes out of a volcano when it erupts

avalanche—a large mass of ice, snow, or earth that suddenly moves down the side of a mountain

biologist—a scientist who studies living things

core—the inner part of Earth that is made of metal, rocks, and melted rock

crater—a hole at the top of a volcano

crust—the thin outer layer of Earth's surface

dormant—not active; dormant volcanoes have not erupted for a very long time

erupt—to suddenly burst; a volcano shoots steam, lava, and ash into the air when it erupts

evacuate—to leave an area during a time of danger

geologist—a scientist who studies how Earth formed and how it changes by examining soil, rocks, rivers, and other landforms

geothermal—relating to the intense heat inside Earth

geyser—an underground spring that shoots hot water and steam through a hole in the ground

hot spring—a place where warm water comes out of the ground

lahar—material that flows down a volcano's slope after water mixes with volcanic debris

lava—the hot, liquid rock that pours out of a volcano when it erupts

magma—melted rock found beneath the surface of Earth

mantle—the layer of super-hot rock that surrounds Earth's core

meteorologist—a person who studies and predicts weather

obsidian—a dark glasslike rock formed by cooling volcanic lava

plate—a large sheet of rock that is a piece of Earth's crust

pressure—the force produced by pressing on something

toxic—poisonous

tsunami—a large, destructive wave caused by an underwater earthquake or volcano

vent—a hole in a volcano; hot ash, steam, and lava blow out of vents from an erupting volcano

volcanology—the study of volcanoes

CRITICAL THINKING USING THE COMMON CORE

On page 5 compare the photos of Mount St. Helens before and after its eruption. Using details from the text, explain why the mountain looked different after the eruption. (Key Ideas and Details)

Think about the words "crust" and "core." Now read page 8 to see how these words describe parts of Earth. How does the diagram help show their meaning? (Craft and Structure)

Look at the photographs of the volcanologists on pages 28 and 29. If you had that job, what signs might you see that would make you warn people to leave the area around a volcano? (Integration of Knowledge and Ideas)

READ MORE

Branley, Franklyn M. *Volcanoes.* Let's-Read-and-Find-Out Science. Stage 2. New York: Collins, 2008.

Gray-Wilburn, Renée. *Volcanoes!* Wild Earth. North Mankato, Minn.: Capstone Press, 2012.

Rusch, Elizabeth. *Volcano Rising.* Watertown, Mass.: Charlesbridge, 2013.

INTERNET SITES

FactHound offers a safe, fun way to find Internet sites related to this book. All of the sites on FactHound have been researched by our staff.

Here's all you do:

Visit *www.facthound.com*

Type in this code: 9781476539348

Super-cool stuff!

Check out projects, games and lots more at
www.capstonekids.com

INDEX